iBooks: 978-1-63199-449-4
Kindle: 978-1-63199-450-0
Google Play: 978-1-63199-451-7
Adobe Digital Editions: 978-1-63199-452-4

Print:
ISBN10: 1-63199-448-4
ISBN13: 978-1-63199-448-7

Energion Publications
P. O. Box 841
Gonzalez, FL 32560

pubs@energion.com
energion.com

Acknowledgments

While this is a short book, it is based on my study and discussions spanning several decades. As a result, numerous people have influenced and shaped my views, starting long before I became a Christian. I want to thank all of them, those who supported me, and those who did not. Everyone played a role in shaping the views I express in this book. And of course, I must thank my friend and editor Henry Neufeld for his efforts and support.

Introduction

Look to the essence of a thing, whether it be a point of doctrine, of practice, or of interpretation.
(Marcus Aurelius Antoninus A.D. 121-180)[1]

For the time will come when people will not tolerate healthy doctrine.
(2 Timothy 4:3)

THE DECADE OF the 1970s brought a great explosion of interest in the inner self. Spiritual awareness and enlightenment were diligently sought after. Many looked to eastern religions such as Zen and Taoism. Others looked to gurus. Some joined communes. Christianity saw a revival with the Jesus People and the Born-Again movement. With all this diversity, many people felt that it really didn't matter which movement you followed as long as you were sincere. Everyone had to seek their own path, and all paths led to God.

One of these religious movements flourished in San Francisco under the guidance of a charismatic leader named Jim. Jim preached all the right things: concern for the sick and underprivileged, help for the poor, and support for minorities. Local politicians liked him because he could be counted on to bring large crowds to rallies. There was even some talk that he had done a few miracles.

---

1   Marcus Aurelius Antoninus, *Meditations* VII, 22

In the midst of all the popularity, a few did voice concern. Jim may have started as a Christian minister back in Indiana, but somewhere along the way he moved away from the teachings found in the book that Christians consider to be inspired by God, and the foundation of their beliefs: The Bible. A few Christians complained about his unorthodox beliefs. Some relatives complained about his total control over family members. Some of those who had attended his church talked of abuse and pressure to raise funds. For the most part these charges were ignored. Jim continued to preach love and social concerns, and continued to attract followers.

All of this changed on November 18, 1978, when United States Congressman Leo Ryan and four others were murdered while investigating reports of abuse at Jonestown, the People's Temple commune in Guyana. When Guyanese troops arrived at Jonestown the next day, they made a grisly discovery – the bodies of 913 people, over 200 of which were children. Most had died from drinking cyanide-laced punch. Jim Jones had been shot through the head, apparently by one of his inner circle.

Those who followed Jim Jones to their deaths in the jungles of Guyana may have been sincere, but their sincerity did not protect them from being wrong about their faith and their leader. Nor were they the only ones who may have been sincere, but wrong. In the middle of the 1990s a total of seventy-four members of The Order of the Solar Temple died in several mass suicides that ended with buildings being set on fire by remote control devices. On March 26, 1997, Marshall Applewhite, convinced thirty-eight of his follower to join him in getting their money together, packing their suitcases, and cleansing their body by drinking citrus juices. The males were castrated; everyone put on new, identical, Nike sneakers and then they committed suicide. All this so they could go to a spaceship that was supposed to be hiding behind the Hale-Bopp comet.[2] These people were certainly sincere – sincere enough to commit suicide for their beliefs – but sincerity is not enough.

Jim Jones may have preached about love, but he denounced the teachings of the Bible. The People's Temple was not a Christian group, even though it was often labeled as such in the press. But

2 http://en.wikipedia.org/wiki/Cult_suicide

if those in the media were wrong to label the People's Temple a Christian group, why? What is a Christian group? In spite of the importance of Christianity to the historical development of Western civilization, many people are surprisingly unaware of even its most basic beliefs. This can be seen in the wide variety of groups that claim to be Christian even when they deny the central teachings that have historically defined Christianity.

For Christians, the foundation for what they believe, or their doctrine, is found in the Bible. In my book Evidence for the Bible, I examine the question of whether the Bible can be trusted to provide this foundation and concluded that it can. Here we will look at some of the key teachings, or doctrines. But before we look at the individual doctrines, we need to examine the charge that defining the basic teachings of the Bible is an impossible task.

<><><><><><><><><><><><><><><><><><><><><><><><><><><><><><><><><><><><><><><>

A MATTER OF INTERPRETATION

It is often claimed that nobody really knows what the Bible says. It is all just a matter of interpretation, with one interpretation being as good as another. While this belief is very common, it is nevertheless false. It is possible to read and understand what the Bible teaches. Yet, if this is true, then why are there so many churches, each claiming to be Christian?

Part of the problem is how one approaches this subject. There are issues and concerns with understanding the Bible, and it is very common to start by outlining all of these problems. When discussing individual teachings, often there is a greater focus on the areas of disagreement and this can leave the incorrect impression that, when it comes to understanding the Bible, there is nothing but problems and disagreements.

It must also be remembered that the Bible describes God's dealings with his creation, and it covers a large number of topics. On the most important teachings, such as who is God, and how we can be saved, the Bible is pretty clear. On the core of these doctrines there is little dispute among Christians. On other teachings, the Bible is not as clear. Sometimes this is because we are

dealing with God, and as created beings we cannot be expected to fully comprehend all that the Creator does. At other times, it is simply because the doctrines are not essential to salvation and are only briefly mentioned. There are also disagreements over how all these teachings fit together. It is on these non-essential doctrines that Christian churches differ.

The Bible is not an esoteric book teaching doctrines that only the initiated can understand. The apostle Paul stated, "We do not write you anything that you cannot read or understand" (2 Corinthians 1:13). If you accept the premise that words have a particular meaning when used in a particular context, the Bible can be understood. If you don't accept this premise, then *ALL* communication becomes impossible. The Bible was written in the everyday language of its time. It was written to convey the truths of God as simply and to as many people as possible.

One source of difficulty is in the fact that, at least for most people, the version of the Bible they read is a translation. Normally this is not much of a problem and the major translations all do a pretty good job of accurately translating the Bible. But there are some inherent problems in translation that cannot be completely avoided. For one there is always a tension between the literal accuracy of a translation and its readability. There is also the problem that the words used to translate a passage do not completely correspond to the original word in all its nuances.

For example, the KJV translation of the sixth commandment ("Thou shalt not kill" [Ex 20:13]) is an acceptable translation, but it often leads to confusion. While the Hebrew word ratsach (רָצַח) can be translated kill, so can seven other Hebrew words. Of these seven words, ratsach is the one that would be closest to the English word murder. Thus, while the KJV translation is okay, the translation in the NIV ("You shall not murder,") is better.

Some people claim that because of problems such as these, everything in the Bible is simply a matter of interpretation. Usually they justify this by challenging the meaning of every word they can. While it is true that some words can have multiple meanings, normally this does not hinder us in communication – that is unless someone does not want to communicate. If I say that I'm going

4

to run down to the store, there would be little doubt about my intentions. If this were a Biblical passage, then the critic would probably question: (1) Whether I was actually going to run? (2) What I meant by down? (3) Was it really a store I was going to, or could it have been a shop? They would then use this ambiguity to ignore the passage altogether, stating that it is too vague to be clearly understood.

Another problem that often ends up making it seem as if the Bible cannot be clearly understood is when statements are cited out of context. It is context that gives meaning to what we say. By taking things out of context, you can make anyone say just about anything. Someone who wanted to misquote me could use the passage at the start of this section and have me say that understanding the Bible is impossible: " ...nobody really knows what the Bible says. It is all just a matter of interpretation, with one interpretation being as good as another." Clearly this is not my position. It is the opposite of my position. Yet this sort of thing happens with the Bible all the time.

While sometimes deliberate, for the most part this is usually done out of ignorance. For many the Bible is just a collection of loosely connected statements, something akin to a smorgasbord of sayings from which one can select out those that agree with what they are trying to demonstrate. Part of this comes from the chapter and verse numbering system developed by Stephen Langton while a professor at the University of Paris, around 1227.[3] Part of this comes from the common practice of teaching children to memorize verses. But for whatever the reason, for many people the Bible exists in their minds as little more than a collection of statements.

While this may be a good description of the book of Proverbs, it does not apply to the other books of the Bible. Rather than loosely connected statements, a great deal of consideration was given to how they were written. The Gospel of John, for example was not haphazardly thrown together, but has the following broad outline to its structure:

---

3 Norman Geilser and William Nix, *A General Introduction to the Bible*, (Chicago, Il: Moody 1986) p. 340

I. The Prologue: Becoming Children of God (1:1-1:18)
   A. The Word and Becoming the Children of God

II. Revelation of Jesus (1:19-10:42)
   A. Jesus is the Word – 7 Days (1:19-51)
   B. Early Ministry – New Replaces Old (2:1-4:54)
   C. Rising Opposition (5:1-10:42)
   D. Conclusion of Section – John the Baptist (10:40-42)

III. Transition – Culmination of Jesus' Public Ministry (11:1-12:50
   A. Jesus' Greatest Miracles – The Raising of Lazarus (11:1-54)
   B. Triumphal Entry (11:55-12:50)
   C. Summation of Public Ministry (12:37-50)

IV. The Work of Jesus (13:1-20:31)
   A. The Last Supper (13:1- 30)
   B. Jesus Prepares His Disciples for His Departure (13:31-17:26)
   C. Passion (18:1-20:31)

V. Epilogue: Loving God Means Serving Others (21:1-25)
   A. Jesus Appears to His Disciples by the Sea (21:1-14)
   B. Do You Love Me? (21:15-24)
   C. The Greatness of Jesus (21:25)

As you can see, the Gospel has two main sections: the first concerns the revelation of who Jesus is, the second his work. Between these is a short transition section. There is also a prologue that introduces the main themes and the epilogue. Internally, each of these sections has its own structural features, which are often very carefully written. For example, the prologue was written in the form of a chiasmus where the various points are counterbalanced in such a way as to build around a key or central point.

1:1-2   Word ⇔ God
  :3   Made everything
   :4-5   Life ⇔ Light
    :6-8   John the Baptist
     :9   True light coming into world
      :10-11   Rejected by the world and his own
       :12a   As many received him
        :12b   He gave them the right to become children of God
       :12c   To as many as believed him
      :13   Chosen by God
     :14   Word became flesh
    :15   John the Baptist
   :16   Received grace instead of grace
  :17   Grace and truth came through Jesus
:18   God (the Word) has revealed God.

Notice in this structure how the various concepts leading to the central point, "He gave them the right to become the children of God," are balanced with corresponding concepts leading away, starting and ending with the Word and God.[4] For example, John the Baptist is mentioned in the fourth point before the center and then again in the fourth point after the center. Such order and structure does not happen by chance. The central statement was not just a random thought tossed in, but its location in the prologue and in this chiastic structure shows that it is a key theme in the Gospel. Nor are such carefully constructed literary features uncommon in the Bible. Granted it takes a lot longer to understand the context of a passage and why the author chose to write a passage

---

4 This structure is based on the original Greek text. The structure is not always found in translations. For example, with regards to the structure of verse 12 a, b, and c referenced above, order is actually reversed in many translations the so that it reads a, c, and b, because that reads better in modern English.

the way they did. But when this is done, often passages that seem vague, unclear, or confusing suddenly become clear.

∞∞∞

GODS MANY AND LORDS MANY

As an example of how context is important to understanding, and avoiding misunderstanding of what the Bible says, let us look at 1 Corinthians 8:5 where Paul writes, "as there be gods many, and lords many" (KJV). Given that one of the key teachings of the Bible is that there is only one god, why would Paul write this? This passage is frequently cited by members of the *Church of Jesus Christ of Latter Day Saints* (Mormons), and others who believe in many gods, to confirm their belief. Stripped from its context and standing alone like this, it certainly does seem to say that there are many gods. When the passage is put into context, we find that the claim that Paul was saying there are actually many gods, is impossible.

1 Corinthians is a letter written by the Apostle Paul to the church that he had started in Corinth. The church was having problems and had some questions, and in this letter Paul is addressing these questions. The section we now refer to as 1 Corinthians 8 was Paul's response to one of these questions and begins, "Now concerning eating food offered to idols..."

This was an issue, because during the first century, many religions sacrificed animals to the various gods. One side effect of all these sacrifices was that it left the temples with a lot of excess meat, which they would then sell. Thus, the question: Was it ok to eat meat that had been sacrificed to a false god? While this was the main question, as Paul's argument develops we find that there was a second and deeper problem that existed in the church: pride.[5] However, here we will focus in on the main part of the argument which mentions "many gods." The key part of Paul's argument reads as follows:

5　Note in particular how Paul begins (1 Corinthians 8:1-4) and ends (1 Corinthians 8:9-13) his argument.

Therefore concerning the eating of things sacrificed to idols, we know that there is no such thing as an idol in the world, and that there is no God but one. For even if there are so-called gods whether in heaven or on earth, as indeed there are many gods and many lords, yet for us there is but one God, the Father, from whom are all things and we exist for Him; and one Lord, Jesus Christ, by whom are all things, and we exist through Him. (1 Corinthians 8:4-6 NASB).

Once put into context, we see that Paul's statement is hardly a ringing endorsement for the belief that there are many gods. Still, Mormons I have talked to try to claim some ambiguity in the passage so as to leave them room to claim that it is all just a matter of interpretation and that their interpretation is just as valid as any other. However, the passage simply does not leave room for the understanding that there are many gods.

In fact, Paul begins his comments about food sacrificed to idols with a very strong statement that there is only one God: "We know that there is no such thing as an idol in the world, and that there is no God but one." Having established this as his premise, he then goes on to acknowledge what would have been obvious to anyone in Corinth during the first century, that there were many "so-called"[6] gods. Corinth had many temples, the most famous being the temple to Aphrodite, goddess of love, which was known for its temple prostitutes. But there were also major temples to Asclepius and Apollo along with several others.

It is in this context we find Paul's statement, in verse 5, "For even if there are so-called gods whether in heaven or on earth, as indeed there are many gods and many lords." The structure here is: For even if A, as there are B. In such a structure B refers back to A, where A is a theoretical, and B is the actual. As such, the "many gods and many lords" of the latter part of this phrase can only refer to the "so-called gods" in the previous part of the statement. He is talking about food sacrifice to idols and he is admitting the fact that people called these idols gods. As if this were not clear enough Paul then goes on to make yet another statement of the Christian belief of monotheism, "yet for us there is but one God."

---

6 Greek word is legomenoi - λεγόμενοι.

9

So when put into context, the passage is not vague at all. It is clear that Paul is referring to the gods to whom the meat in question was sacrificed and his point is that these are false gods and that they do not exist; "there is no such thing." It does not matter whether or not the meat was sacrificed to something that does not exist and therefore it is okay to eat it. His argument can be broken down as follows:

There is only one God.
Our God is the true God (implied premise)
Therefore, all other gods are nothing.

If the other gods are nothing, then the meat is not defiled.
If the meat is not defiled, then it is okay to eat.

To try and claim that Paul is really saying there are many gods not only misses the context, it destroys the argument that Paul is making, which depends on these other gods being nothing. If the other gods do exist, then Paul's reasoning that the meat is okay to eat falls apart. So whether one is looking at the statements in context, or the flow of the argument that Paul is making, it is not "just a matter of interpretation" whether or not Paul supports the belief that many gods exist.

Again, I am not claiming that every passage in the Bible is as clear as this one. Sometimes we simply do not know enough about the actual context to know for sure exactly what is being said, or we do not know for sure exactly how a passage should be translated and thus there is room for legitimate disagreement. Since the areas of disagreement tend to get a lot more discussion than the areas of agreement, this leads to the perception that everything is simply a matter of interpretation. But it is fallacious to conclude that because some passages are unclear, all passages are unclear. Not everything is subject to interpretation. In a great many areas, the Bible is clear.

A major problem that leads to a lot of confusion concerns one's initial approach to the Bible. While very common, the main question when trying to understand the Bible should not be: What

does it mean to me? It makes little difference what I think or you think a passage should say. The real question that matters is: What was the author trying to say? When there is a dispute over what a certain passage says, then read it for yourself, in context, seeking the intent of the author. Often this will settle the issue.

For those times when a statement is still unclear, biblical scholars use principles to try to understand them. Most of these rules are simply common sense. For example, if there are two statements on a subject, one is clear in what it says while the other is somewhat vague, then you interpret the vague statements in light of the clear one. Another rule is to never base a doctrine on a single statement, especially one that is vague, and then interpret the rest of the Bible to fit it.

When these simple principles of interpretation are employed, the teachings of the Bible are clear, at least for the central doctrines we will look at shortly. On these central beliefs there is very little dispute. In fact, it has been these doctrines that have defined Christianity as a religion. Groups that accept these doctrines are considered to be Christian groups. Those who do not accept these doctrines cannot be considered Christians, at least not in any historical sense.

Some may consider it to be judgmental and arrogant to say who is or is not a Christian simply because they do or do not accept a particular doctrine or belief. First, let it be clear that we are talking about classifying groups based on beliefs. After all, if there is a difference between being a Christian, Jew, Muslim, Buddhist, or Hindu, does it not mean that Christians must have some distinct beliefs that can be contrasted with these other religions? Second we are not talking about an individual's relationship with God. This is a spiritual matter that only God can judge, for only He knows what is truly in a person's heart. We may be able to get a good indication by the person's actions or beliefs but we cannot judge the heart. We will return to the question of individuals at the end of this book.

Groups, on the other hand, do not have personal relationships with God. What defines a religious group are the beliefs of the group. If we were to be completely non-judgmental, then we would have to conclude that any group that claimed to be Chris-

tian was so, regardless of what they believed. This would render the term "Christian" completely meaningless. Should we consider a group that believed in child sacrifice to be a Christian group? Would this make child sacrifice a legitimate expression of the teachings of Christ? Clearly not. So, the question is not should a line be drawn that defines Christianity, but where do we draw that line.

If no line is drawn, Christianity becomes a completely meaningless term that could be applied to any group or any action from the most divine to the most depraved. If, on the other hand, we compose a long and extensive list of doctrines that must be accepted in order for a group to be considered Christian, then we would indeed be arrogant and judgmental, restricting Christianity only to those groups that agreed with us in every little detail. The doctrines that define Christianity should be limited to those expressly taught in the Bible as essential and held by the vast majority of those claiming to be Christian down through the centuries.

ESSENTIAL TEACHINGS

There are basically four beliefs that have defined Christianity as a religion for nearly 2000 years. From these four beliefs flow all of the other teachings and beliefs of Christianity. These beliefs can be briefly summarized as follows:

- The nature of God is best represented by the doctrine of the Trinity: that there is only one God but within the one God exists three persons, the Father, the Son, and the Holy Spirit, all of whom are God.

- Jesus Christ is the only Son of God, who died on the cross for our sins, and he rose again bodily in victory over death.

- Man is a sinner in need of salvation, which is made possible by the death of Jesus, and can only be gained by grace through faith.

❧ The Bible is the inspired word of God.

Most people have heard of these doctrines at one time or another. Still, though these teachings have been around for nearly two thousand years, there has been a lot of confusion concerning them. A large part of this confusion is caused by semi-Christian religions[7] that describe their beliefs using the same terminology that Christians do. While they may use the same words, they have changed the meanings so that they refer to something completely different.

I have talked to many Mormons who would agree with some of the above statements.[8] Yet the teachings of Latter Day Saints on each of these doctrines are vastly different from what Christianity has historically taught.[9] These Mormons were not trying to be deceptive, but rather their Church has redefined these terms. When a Latter Day Saint uses the term "Son of God" as defined by their church,[10] they mean something different than the historic Christian understanding of this term. Because of this, a Mormon and a Christian can both believe that Jesus is the Son of God and still be in disagreement as to who Jesus is.

So that there is no confusion as to what the basic teachings of Christianity are, let us take a closer look at each of these doctrines. This will not, by any means, be an exhaustive survey.[11] Hopefully

7   The term *semi-Christian religion* is used here in a technical sense and is not intended to be a prejudicial term. The term simply refers to a group which, although they claim to be Christian, rejects some or all of the doctrines and teachings which have historically defined Christianity as a religion.

8   Most Mormons would probably agree with points 2 - 4.

9   There are many good books on the differences between the Latter Days Saints doctrine and Christian doctrine. Two good books are: Martin, Walter, *The Kingdom of the Cults* (Minneapolis: Bethany Fellowship, 1977) and Tanner, Jerald and Sandra, *The Changing World of Mormonism* (Chicago: Moody Press, 1980)

10 Mormon doctrine teaches that Jesus is literally a son of God the Father and Mother, created out of their union. Since Mormon doctrine also teaches that we were created out of this union, Jesus is literally our spirit brother. For the historical Christian teaching see the section on Jesus Christ, later in this chapter.

11 There are many excellent books out on the doctrines of Christianity. A very good place to start would be: Walter Martin, Essential Christianity (Santa

it will be enough to clarify these doctrines and demonstrate why Christians believe them.

∞∞∞

THE TRINITY

One of the foundational beliefs of any religion is its beliefs about God. Christianity declares that God does exist, that He created the universe, and that He continues to interact with His creation today. Through revelation, God has shown Himself to exist as what has historically come to be called the Trinity.[12] The doctrine of the Trinity teaches that there is only one God, but that within the nature of the one God there exist three distinct, separate, and equal persons, the Father, the Son, and the Holy Spirit.

While there is no single statement in the Bible that states "God exists as the Trinity," the doctrine is clearly taught. The Trinity is the only explanation that takes into account all of the teachings of the Bible concerning God. Put simply, if the Bible states that there are three separate persons – the Father, the Son, and the Holy Spirit – that each of these persons is God, and that there is only one God, what explanation would fit other than the doctrine of the Trinity?

Few would disagree with the fact that the Father, the Son, and the Holy Spirit are three separate persons.[13] Matthew demonstrates this quite clearly in his account of the baptism of Jesus. Just after John the Baptist baptized Jesus in the river Jordan, the Father spoke from heaven saying, "This is my Son, whom I love. I am pleased

---

Ana, CA: Vision House, 1980). For those who wish a more in depth study: J. Oliver Buswell, *A Systematic Theology of the Christian Religion*. (Grand Rapids, MI: Zondervan, 1962) or Millard J. Erickson, Christian Theology (Grand Rapids, MI: Baker, 1985)

12 The word Trinity does not appear in either the New or Old Testaments. It is a Latin term, first used by Tertullian in the later part of the second century to describe the teachings of the Bible about the nature of God.

13 Some, like the United Pentecostal Church do dispute the existence of three Persons, and instead claim that Jesus sometimes appears in the role of the Father or in the role of the Holy Spirit. Because of this, and other reasons, they were expelled from the Assembly of God in the early part of this century.

with him!" At the same time, the Holy Spirit descended on Jesus "like a dove" (Matthew 3:16-17).

We can see in this account that all three persons of the Trinity are mentioned as being in different locations at the same time, which demonstrates that they are three separate persons. When Jesus stated that His will was in subjection to the will of His Father (Luke 22:42), He demonstrated the existence of two separate wills, and therefore, two separate persons. In John 8:17-18 Jesus said that He and His Father were two witnesses. Also, unless you believe that Jesus was praying to himself, the prayers of Jesus to the Father (John 17) demonstrate that Jesus and the Father are different persons.

That the Father is God is clearly and directly stated in, for example, Peter's use of the phrase "God the Father" (2 Peter 1:17). The deity of Jesus Christ is also an inescapable teaching of the Bible. John opens his Gospel with his description of the Word: "In the beginning was the Word, and the Word was with God, and the Word was God" (John 1:1). John goes on to identify the Word as Jesus Christ (John 1:14-15, 30-31).

Jesus is not only God, but He is the God of the Old Testament. When Moses was on Mount Sinai, he asked God His name so he would be able to say who had sent him to free the Israelites. God answered by saying "I AM WHO I AM," and told Moses to say that "I AM" had sent him (Exodus 3:14). In the book of Isaiah, and especially chapters 40-55, God refers to himself as "I am he" (see for example Isaiah 43:10). When these passages were later translated into Greek (the language of the New Testament) they were translated as the Greek words ego eimi (ἐγὼ εἰμί) which also means "I am."

One day Jesus had a dispute in the temple with the Jewish leaders who were pointing out that they were children of Abraham. They asked him, "Who do you think you are?" Jesus responded, "Truly, I tell all of you emphatically, before there was an Abraham, I am!" (John 8:53-58). Here Jesus referred to himself as ego eimi (I am), exactly the same Greek words used by God in the Greek version of Isaiah. At that point the Jewish leaders picked up stones in order to kill Jesus. There are only two choices: either they wanted to stone Jesus for improper grammar (I am instead of I was), or

because he was claiming to be I AM, the God who had appeared to Moses and Isaiah.

During another dispute in the temple, the Jews once again picked up some stones in an attempt to kill Jesus. But Jesus stopped them, asking, "I've shown you many good actions from my Father. For which of them are you going to stone me?" The Jews replied that they were not going to stone him for any of the works that Jesus had performed. Instead they said, "because you, a mere man, are making yourself God!" (John 10:31-33). Clearly the Jews understood the claims that Jesus made about himself.

There are at least eight passages in the New Testament in which the deity of Jesus Christ seems to be directly stated.[14] Paul wrote to Titus, a disciple he had left on the island of Crete to organize a church: "As we wait for the blessed hope and glorious appearance of our great God and Savior, Jesus the Messiah" (Titus 2:13). In the book of Hebrews, God the Father says of His Son, "Your throne, O God, is forever and ever" (Hebrews 1:8). The Bible teaches that Jesus is God the Son.

Although the deity of the Holy Spirit is not expressed as often as the deity of Jesus Christ, it is still clearly set forth. In the book of Acts, Luke describes for us the situation in the early church. In one instance two converts, Ananias and Sapphira, attempted to deceive the church. Peter confronted them, saying, they lied "to the Holy Spirit" and that they didn't just lie to them, "but also to God!" (Acts 5:1-4).

The Bible teaches three persons – the Father, the Son and the Holy Spirit – are God. Normally, this would lead us to conclude that the Bible teaches polytheism, the belief in many gods. This is what the Mormons have concluded, believing that the Father, Son and Holy Spirit are three gods.[15] The Bible, however, teaches that there is only one God.

---

14 John 1:1, John 1:18, John 20:28, Romans 9:5, Titus 2:13, 2 Peter 1:1, Hebrews 1:8, 1 John 5:20.

15 The Latter Day Saint doctrine could also be classified as henotheism, the belief in many gods with the worship of one, for they see the Father, Son, and Holy Spirit as a single "Godhead." Mormon doctrine teaches there are many gods and Mormon males will, if they follow the teaching of the church, become gods themselves, but they worship only one "Godhead."

That the Old Testament teaches there is only one God can hardly be questioned. One of the distinguishing marks of the Jewish religion is its strict monotheism. This strict monotheism is carried into the New Testament as well. Jesus referred to the "praise that comes from the only God" (John 5:44), and as we have already seen, Paul stated: "We know that an idol is nothing at all in the world and that there is no God but one" (1 Corinthians 8:4). James said of the belief in one God that, "even the demons believe that – and shudder" (James 2:19).

The main problem with the Trinity is that it is understandably difficult to comprehend because it is beyond our realm of experience. Because of this, many analogies are used to help understand the Trinity. One analogy I often use is that of lines in different dimensions. In a one-dimensional universe, only length would exist. The only types of objects that could exist (besides a single point) would be lines. There would be no such thing as a two-lined object, because as can be seen in Figure 3.1 if two lines are joined, they simply become a single, longer line. In a one-dimensional universe, the number of lines is equal to the number of objects.

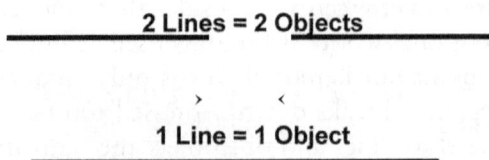

1 Dimension

2 Lines = 2 Objects

1 Line = 1 Object

Figure 3.1

If we add a second dimension (width), lines can now be joined at angles to make objects other than just lines. For example, three lines could be joined end to end to create a triangle as seen in Figure 3.2.

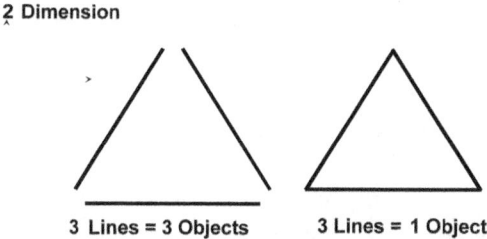

2 Dimension

3 Lines = 3 Objects   3 Lines = 1 Object

Figure 3.2

A triangle is a single object that is made up of three distinct lines. From a one-dimensional point of view, this makes no sense. It is impossible for three lines to be in a single object and still be three separate lines. From a two-dimensional point of view, three separate lines and one object is no problem at all.

Appling this to our understanding of the Trinity, we see that while the concept of three separate persons existing as a single God may seem impossible, when we consider that God is not limited to our 3-dimensional world, it no longer seems improbable. It is important to point out here that this is only an analogy, and as with all analogies, it breaks down if pressed too far. In this case while you have three lines and one object the individual lines are only part of the object. Individual lines are just that, individual lines. Only together are they a triangle. Yet the three persons of the Trinity are not parts of God, they are God.

Fundamentally, this conception of God is beyond our ability to understand, because it is a conception of God that is completely beyond our experience. Analogies can help to some extent, but they remain that, analogies. In short, if you think that you really understand the Trinity, then that is a good indication that you don't.

Some people have told me that the doctrine of the Trinity only proves that the Bible contradicts itself. To them, the doctrine of the Trinity is simply the result of theologians trying to reconcile those contradictions; and as a result they come up with something completely incomprehensible. This argument might have some validity if one writer claimed that both the Father and Jesus were God, while a different writer claimed there is only one God. But this is not what we find. The doctrine of the Trinity is supported throughout much of the New Testament, and to some extent even in the Old Testament.[16] It would be no problem at all to restrict ourselves to a single author (like Paul or John) and still demonstrate the doctrine of the Trinity. Rather than a demonstration of how the Bible contradicts itself, the doctrine of the Trinity demonstrates the harmony of the authors. Even for such a complex and difficult doctrine, the different authors are in complete agreement with one another.

Throughout history, the doctrine of the Trinity has been one of the most controversial of the basic teachings of Christianity. This is due mainly to the fact that the doctrine of the Trinity is beyond our ability to fully comprehend. We can know that there are three persons and yet only one God, but we cannot understand it. As the noted author C. S. Lewis stated, this was:

> ... one of the reasons I believe Christianity. It is a religion you could not have guessed. If it offered us just the kind of universe we had always expected, I should feel we were making it up.[17]

The fact that we cannot understand the nature of God should not be too troubling, for the creation cannot really expect to understand the creator. When we find that the Christian doctrine of the Trinity is beyond our comprehension, this should be evidence for the veracity of Christianity, as it was for C. S. Lewis.

As in so many instances, this is really a Catch-22 situation. Many critics claim that since the Trinity is beyond our comprehen-

---

16 For examples of the Trinity in the Old Testament see Genesis 1 and Proverbs 30:1-4.

17 C S Lewis, *Mere Christianity* (New York, New York: Macmillan, 1952) pp. 47-8

sion, it does not make sense, and must be false. If the Christian concept of God were to be a nice neat package, one that could be easily understood, it would be cited as proof that people had created God in their own image, and again it must be false. Either way, Christianity will be criticized.

◇◇

JESUS CHRIST

Central to the beliefs of Christianity is the nature and work of Jesus Christ. As we have seen, Christianity teaches that Jesus Christ is God the Son, who took on the form of a man and lived among His creation (John 1:1-3 and John 1:14, Philippians 2:6-8). The story of His life, death, and resurrection are fairly well known and we need not go into great detail here. What often is not appreciated is the importance of these events to the Christian faith.

I have talked to many people who believe that Jesus was a good man, or that the world would be better off if more people would follow His moral teachings. But the heart of the Christian faith is not the moral teachings of Jesus. While important, they are only secondary. If Jesus had been primarily a moral teacher, then this would not have required Him to be God. There would have been no need for the virgin birth. The miracles He did would have served little purpose. Finally, His death would only have been a tragic end to a promising ministry.

Paul tells us that the death of Jesus was not a tragic end. Instead, it was a central part of Christ's purpose on earth. Paul writes:

> For I passed on to you *the most important* points that I received: The Messiah died for our sins according to the Scriptures, he was buried, he was raised on the third day according to the Scriptures—and is still alive! (1 Corinthians 15:3-4 italics added)

Christianity is not simply a nice set of moral teachings. Christianity teaches that man is a sinner in need of salvation. Christ came to provide the means for that salvation through His death on the cross. That Jesus is God is important because only God could bear the punishment for all of our sins. The virgin birth was im-

portant as the means by which God entered into the world. The miracles testified that Jesus is the Messiah.

As we saw earlier, Jesus claimed to be the God who had appeared to Moses in the Old Testament. If He is not God, then as C. S. Lewis pointed out,

> He would either be a lunatic – on a level with the man who says he is a poached egg – or else he would be the Devil of Hell. You must make your choice. Either this man was, and is the Son of God: or else a madman or something worse. You can shut Him up for a fool, you can spit at Him and kill Him as a demon; or you can fall at His feet and call Him Lord and God. But let us not come with any patronizing nonsense about His being a great human teacher. He has not left that open to us. He did not intend to.[18]

As Paul stated in his letter to the church in the Greek city of Corinth, the heart of Christianity is not the moral teachings of Jesus, but his victory over death in the resurrection (1 Corinthians 15:3-4). Greek philosophy of the time taught that only the soul was immortal, not the body. Because of this, there were some in the church at Corinth who thought that they could discard the resurrection as unimportant and unnecessary baggage. In response to this Paul wrote:

> ... and if the Messiah has not been raised, then our message means nothing and your faith means nothing ... and if the Messiah has not been raised, your faith is worthless and you are still imprisoned by your sins. Yes, even those who have died believing in the Messiah are lost. If we have set our hopes on the Messiah in this life only, we deserve more pity than any other people. (1 Corinthians 15:14, 17-19)

The Bible teaches that not only is Jesus God the Son, but that He became a man and lived among His creation. He died on the cross for the sins of the world and rose from the dead three days later. This is the Jesus of the Bible.

---

18 Lewis, *Mere,* p. 56

Christ died for our sins, but how do we take advantage of that? How can we know that we will go to heaven? Many people hope that they are good enough to go to heaven, or at least they hope that they are not bad enough to go to hell. But the Bible does not teach that we should just hope; we should know. The apostle John wrote: "I have written these things to you who believe in the name of the Son of God so that you may know that you have eternal life." (1 John 5:13).

How can anyone know if they are good enough? How could anyone have any sense of assurance that they will go to heaven? The simple answer is that they can't. Based on the statements of the Bible, the only assurance we can have is that when we are judged we will not pass the test. Instead, we will all fail miserably. Paul wrote in his letter to the church in Rome that "all have sinned and continue to fall short of God's glory" (Romans 3:23) and "Therefore God will not justify any human being by means of the actions prescribed by the Law, for through the Law comes the full knowledge of sin." (Romans 3:20). Anyone who has ever committed even a single sin will not meet God's perfect standard.

But what is sin? Sin as a concept has fallen in popularity and is currently out of fashion. Even the concept of evil is rarely used any longer as an explanation for the actions of people. If someone goes on a killing spree, savagely butchering innocent bystanders, there will be a flood of explanations as to why they may have done it. These explanations will include almost every possible reason, with the exception of one: that the killer was an evil person. As a society we have, to a large extent, lost the ability to pass moral judgments. Good and evil no longer exist. Today there is only good and not so good.

Christianity not only accepts the existence of evil, but teaches that humans are (from God's point of view) basically evil. This does not mean that people cannot be good. This is a teaching about underlying inclinations. People have to be taught to be good. Anyone who has raised children knows they are naturally rebellious.

Just Fucking Vote

by Ralph Lane